WORDS *of* HOPE *and* HEALING

THE
VULNERABILITY
of GRIEF

Finding *the* Courage *to*
Authentically Mourn

Alan D. Wolfelt, Ph.D.

Companion
PRESS

An imprint of the Center for Loss and Life Transition | Fort Collins, Colorado

Companion Press is an imprint of the Center for Loss and Life Transition, 3735 Broken Bow Road, Fort Collins, Colorado 80526.

28 27 26 25 24 23   6 5 4 3 2 1

ISBN: 978-1-61722-329-7

CONTENTS

WELCOME

"What happens when people open their hearts? They get better."
— Haruki Murakami

For the lucky among us, grief is a bittersweet necessity.

Lucky? Yes. Because deep grief comes only to those who deeply love. And love is the most rewarding experience human beings are privileged to have in our brief stays here on earth.

If you have found your way to this book, you have no doubt suffered a significant life loss. Maybe someone you love has died, and your heart has been torn apart. Or perhaps you have suffered a different but still painful life loss. It's important to acknowledge that deep grief also arises from a wide range of common losses, such as divorce, estrangement, health problems, and many others.

Whatever your loss, I am glad you picked up this book. While love is indeed lucky, the grief resulting from it is so very hard. In fact, I believe there is nothing more difficult. Grief can feel unbearably painful for a long time.

C.S. Lewis, one of my favorite authors, said that "to love at all is to be vulnerable." What he meant, of course, is that to love is to be exposed to loss and pain. In other words, love is risky. You have probably learned this truth all too well.

But in this little book you will also learn that being vulnerable is a good thing. Just as you made yourself vulnerable by loving, you must now also make yourself vulnerable in mourning.

Together we will explore the transformative power of authentically encountering, exploring, and expressing your grief. This will take fortitude. So we will also talk through ways to muster the courage it takes to share your deepest emotions outside of yourself, one small step at a time.

Over the coming months and years, practicing vulnerability in grief will help you heal.

Adopting a vulnerable orientation to life will also help you experience a richer, fuller, more meaning-filled existence. Truth be told, I believe that vulnerability can be the key to unlocking your potential, your hopes, and your joys. Let's begin.

PART ONE

GRIEF AND VULNERABILITY

*"There is no intensity of love or feeling that does not involve
the risk of crippling hurt. It is a duty to take this risk,
to love and feel without defense or reserve."*

— William S. Burroughs

Let's start by reviewing what I mean by the foundational concepts in this book: grief, mourning, and vulnerability.

Grief is the internal response to loss. It is everything you think and feel inside of you after a loss. It is your internal experience of a loss that happened outside of you. It is your brain's and body's and soul's struggle to come to terms with the hard-to-believe, painful new reality.

The word "grief" comes to us from the Latin words *gravare*, which means "to make heavy," and *gravis*, which means "a heavy burden." Grief is natural and normal. And it is necessary as a means of transitioning to a new normal. But it is also heavy and difficult.

Mourning is expressing your grief outside of yourself in some way. When you cry, you are mourning. When you talk to a friend about your loss, you are mourning. Writing about your loss in a journal, participating in a support group, making art that captures your feelings—these are also mourning actions.

Mourning results in a lightening of the heaviness of grief. It is a movement of unburdening and release. Mourning is the external response to loss, and it, too, is normal and necessary.

Vulnerability means being exposed to uncertainty, and thus, possible harm. The word vulnerability comes to us from the Latin for "wound, hurt, injure."

To make yourself vulnerable is to do the opposite of protecting yourself. When you protect yourself, you create barriers and shields that safeguard you from harm. Common emotional shields include denial, secrecy, and disengagement. On the other hand, when you allow yourself to be vulnerable, you take steps to consciously, proactively lower—and even drop—those shields. You intentionally practice healthy authenticity and self-disclosure.

THE NATURAL VULNERABILITY OF GRIEF AND MOURNING
Grief makes us feel vulnerable.

Grief is the result of an emotional and spiritual injury. Such injuries make us feel vulnerable because when we are wounded, we are naturally tender and laid low. You've heard the phrase "kick a person when they're down." Loss brings us down and makes us feel more vulnerable to normal life struggles and potential additional losses and hardships.

Mourning tends to make us feel vulnerable, too. Why? Because when we express our grief externally, we are quite literally turning ourselves inside out. We are exposing our soft inner selves to the outside world. We are sharing our deepest, most tender feelings and truths.

Another way to look at it is that when we mourn, we are wearing our hearts on our sleeves. And that is a vulnerable place for our hearts to be.

WHAT VULNERABILITY FEELS LIKE

Vulnerability feels like openness to danger—to be exposed. Picture a house without a roof or a turtle without a shell. To be vulnerable is to be susceptible to the elements. To be vulnerable is to be defenseless.

This is why vulnerability typically feels like fear. When we are vulnerable, we know that we are exposed to potential harm. We are aware that our shields are down, and bad things can and probably will happen.

And so, we are taught from a young age not to allow ourselves to be vulnerable but instead protect ourselves. That's why tears are seen as a sign of weakness and standing up to bullies is viewed as a strength. That's why when we admit mistakes, we may be punished instead of rewarded. That's why we may be teased or judged for expressing tender feelings in lieu of the preferred responses of asserting ourselves confidently or keeping our feelings to ourselves.

To protect ourselves from the perceived dangers of vulnerability, we often resort to the following defensive behaviors instead:

- We put on a false front.
- We don't divulge our truest feelings.
- We keep a stiff upper lip.
- We don't share our more tender emotions.
- We don't ask for everything we truly want and need.
- We avoid candor and closeness.
- We run away from intimacy.
- We retreat to numbness, stoicism, and denial.
- We practice perfectionism.
- We champion resilience over vulnerability.
- We adopt toxic positivity, paste on a smile, and "carry on."

If you see yourself in some of the behaviors in this list, rest assured that you're not alone. Our culture has historically misunderstood the paradoxical strengths of vulnerability.

That's why this little book explores a new and better way of being.

VULNERABILITY AND TOXIC POSITIVITY

It's good to be positive, right? To be optimistic and upbeat?

Positivity is the practice of looking at the bright side of a situation. That sounds like a fine idea! Trouble is, positivity is often a form of denial. When that happens, it should be labeled "toxic positivity."

Toxic positivity is pretending that it's always better to focus on the good in any circumstance rather than spend time and energy exploring the more naturally difficult, dark feelings associated with painful life experiences.

In toxic positivity, vulnerability is assigned the role of the bad guy. If you're being toxically positive, you're being "strong" and putting on a sunny demeanor even when you feel bad inside. To borrow a phrase from the musical group R.E.M., we "shiny, happy people" too often forget that loss is a normal and even common human experience that requires grief and mourning.

Perhaps the most important truth I have learned in my four decades as a grief counselor and educator is this: the process of grief and mourning is necessary. If we are attached to someone or some thing, we will absolutely grieve when our relationship with that person or thing is threatened or severed. We will experience painful, distressing thoughts and feelings inside of us. What's more, we will need to express those thoughts and feelings, day by day for as long as it takes. This will help us understand and integrate the loss, and over time, begin to heal.

Toxic positivity tries to deny the need for grief and mourning. But denying hard truths in grief and suppressing genuine thoughts and feelings only lead to what I call "carried grief." Carried grief is grief that has not been fully acknowledged and mourned, which is why I also call it "unembarked mourning."

Carried grief may be locked away, but it's still there. Carried grief is insidious. It is so dangerous because it's a common, invisible cause of long-term wellness issues that negatively affect quality of life. In my work with grieving people, I have many times found carried grief to be at the root of struggles with anxiety, depression, substance use disorders, intimacy, and more. It mutes your divine spark—that essential flame inside you that gives your life meaning and purpose—and it causes many people to, in essence, die while they are still alive.

So let's remember that while there are certainly times and places for positivity in our lives, there are also many, many times and places for grief, mourning, and vulnerability.

PART TWO

RETHINKING VULNERABILITY

"Vulnerability is the birthplace of connection and the path to the feeling of worthiness."
— Brené Brown

It turns out that vulnerability in grief isn't the bad guy after all.

In fact, vulnerability is the good guy.

Why? Because vulnerability is fundamentally about honesty and connection. And with the possible exception of white lies meant to spare others' feelings, honesty and connection are always the best path in grief and in life.

Remember the list of ways in which we commonly protect ourselves from vulnerability? Here they are again, but next to each I've added the honest, vulnerable alternative.

In grief, the honest, vulnerable orientation is the one that will get you where you want to go. In contrast, the protective, dishonest orientation will potentially keep you stuck and suffering from the repercussions of carried grief.

THE VULNERABLE ORIENTATION TO LIFE

PROTECTIVE, DISHONEST ORIENTATION	HONEST, VULNERABLE ORIENTATION
We put on a false front.	We present ourselves to the world as we really are, warts and all.
We don't divulge our truest feelings.	We share our truest feelings openly and proactively.
We keep a stiff upper lip.	We allow ourselves to be sad and emotional when feelings arise.
We don't share our more tender emotions.	We share all our emotions, including the tender ones.
We don't ask for everything we truly want and need.	We feel comfortable and empowered to ask for everything we truly want and need.
We avoid candor and closeness.	We are always genuine, which brings us closer to others.
We run away from intimacy.	We move toward intimacy.
We retreat to numbness, stoicism, and denial.	We choose tenderness, expression, and truth-seeking.
We practice perfectionism.	We are human, and we make mistakes. We live with a growth mindset and generously forgive mistakes in ourselves and others.
We champion resilience over vulnerability.	We know that vulnerability is essential to true resilience.
We adopt toxic positivity, paste on a smile, and "carry on."	We cultivate hope while still giving our full attention to difficult experiences and feelings as they arise.

The Vulnerability of Grief

Notice that the work of mourning—again, openly and honestly expressing your inner grief outside of yourself, no matter what it includes—inhabits the right side of the chart. When you are mourning, you are being honest and vulnerable. You are presenting your soft inner self to the world. You are sharing your truest feelings. You are asking for help and support. You are creating intimacy with others. You are allowing yourself to be perfectly imperfect. You are giving attention to your difficult experiences and feelings.

You can't love without being vulnerable, and you can't mourn without being vulnerable, either. One purpose of this book is to help you understand that while you may be able to grieve inside without being vulnerable, it's a terrible, life-restricting choice to keep that grief inside and present a false, invulnerable façade to the world.

CONGRUENCE AND TABOOS

Psychologists sometimes talk about a concept called "congruence." Congruence means that your outer words and behaviors align with your inner feelings and thoughts. Said another way, the outside matches the inside.

That's what vulnerability is. It's congruent. Congruence is essential because it feels right. It's truthful and genuine. If you've ever lied about something important and then felt guilty about it, you know what I'm talking about here. That's because incongruence feels wrong. It's withholding and dishonest.

Think about how you are at times invited to be dishonest about how you truly feel. Someone asks you, "How are you?" You respond, "I'm fine. And you?" "I'm fine too." You lie, they lie, we all run the risk of lying to defend against our genuine thoughts and feelings.

Yet, when it comes to mourning, only honesty works. Yes, it takes courage to be fully honest about your grief, to be vulnerable enough to show others what's inside you. But grief and mourning are not shameful. Any shame you might feel about authentically mourning is a result of unhealthy cultural taboos and stigmas surrounding grief.

Too often, our culture promotes the left side of the chart on page 10. It teaches us that armoring ourselves with denial and dishonesty is the right way to live. When we experience loss and grief, we are encouraged to keep a stiff upper lip, get over it, and move on. For many people, death is a taboo subject. So are grief and mourning.

However, in recent years, I have been gratified to see that our culture is becoming more aware of the need for congruency. Talking about feelings is now more encouraged. Mental health is now seen by many as the crucial element of holistic health it is. Still, while taboos and stigmas are falling away, they are far from gone. So if you encounter stigmas about vulnerability, grief, and mourning—in yourself or others—remember that progress is slow and that you can choose to be among those who practice and model healthy, honest emotionality and empathetic support.

CHOOSING OTHERS WITH WHOM TO BE VULNERABLE

In my own grief journeys and in the lives of the mourners I have been privileged to companion, I have discovered that in general, you can take all the people in your life and divide them into thirds when it comes to the capacity for grief support.

About a third of the people in your life will turn out to be neutral in response to your expressions of grief. While they may still be good companions for non-grief-related activities in your life, they are not equipped to be empathetic grief supporters. Or they may say, "If you need me, just let me know"—but then you won't hear from them again.

Another third of the people in your life will be harmful to you in your efforts to mourn and heal. While they are usually not setting out to intentionally hurt you, they may judge you, they may shame you, they may try to take your grief away from you, and they may pull you off the path to healing. You will feel worse after you spend time in their company. Avoid this third as you begin to practice vulnerability in grief.

But the final third of the people in your life will turn out to be truly empathetic helpers. They will have a desire to be present to you as you authentically mourn. They will truly listen and try to understand you and your unique thoughts and feelings about your life losses. They will be willing to bear witness to your pain and suffering without feeling the need to give advice or stop you from expressing it. They will believe in your capacity to heal.

While you may find that the people in your life divide up into different proportions than thirds, start by seeking out the friends and family members who fall into this last group. As you grow more practiced and confident at authentically mourning, you may become more at ease at being vulnerable in the presence of the first third. And if you work your way into becoming a vulnerability master, you may ultimately find it rewarding to model healthy vulnerability for the second group. Your mentorship may even end up softening the defenses of the most protective-oriented people, helping them open to the practice and benefits of vulnerability themselves.

BUILDING TRUST AND INTIMACY

Healthy vulnerability takes building trust with the empathetic helpers in your life. If you already have close, mutually trusting relationships with some people, you can probably begin practicing vulnerability in grief in their presence without any additional groundwork. But if you don't have honest, close relationships, you'll need to work toward that.

Trust and vulnerability go hand in hand. After all, when you're being vulnerable in someone's presence, you're entrusting them with your heart, and vice versa. If someone isn't already your close confidant, you may even want to ask permission before baring your soul. "I need to talk to someone about this anger I've been experiencing," you might say. "Is it OK with you if I share a little?" Overtly securing consent in this way can sometimes be appropriate and help build and ensure trust and confidentiality.

In general, trust is built in a relationship through regular and positive interaction, mutual consideration, and good follow through. Being someone who others can count on and want to spend time with is foundational to trust and intimacy.

Of course, a compassionate, grief-informed counselor is someone you can hopefully trust with your most tender thoughts and feelings. I recommend grief counseling to anyone who needs a safe space in which to mourn openly. Even if you have trusted, close friends and family members who are supportive of your need to authentically mourn, a grief counselor can be an essential part of your care network. If it feels appropriate for you, I urge you to consider exploring a supportive counseling relationship.

Sharing your grief with others can be challenging, but it is also rewarding. In fact, deep human bonds and connections are often built on this type of vulnerability. True friendships and love require it. You will find that being open and honest about your grief invites openness and honesty in others. It also activates empathy. As the shields come down, mutual understanding and support can flow back and forth.

ALLOWING YOURSELF TO LOOK FOOLISH

In my decades as a grief counselor, I have learned that one of the most common fears grieving people have about expressing their true thoughts and feelings is the loss of control. They are often afraid that if they let some of their genuine feelings out, the floodgates will open and they will be unable to prevent themselves from breaking down, sobbing, and wailing. They're apprehensive about sharing thoughts that might reveal them to be overly dependent, weak, crazy, or bad.

It's an understandable fear, but note that it lives on the left side of the chart on page 10. Keeping a stiff upper lip and not expressing tender, authentic feelings are part of the protective, dishonest orientation to life. And the only reason we as a culture adhere to such conventions is that we are emotion-phobic and grief-avoidant, which, as I have noted, is not a healthy way to live.

It's OK to break down in front of others. It's OK to wail and let your guard down. It's OK to seem out of control and "foolish." In fact, all of these behaviors are good whenever they are true expressions of what you're feeling inside. Remember, congruency is healthy. Honesty is healthy. Vulnerability is healthy.

I dream of the day when remaining stoic and living on the left side of the chart are what is widely considered "looking foolish." That's the day when we will have arrived at a healthy understanding of vulnerability and emotionality. You and I may not live to see this day, but I do believe the tide is slowly turning. And we can take comfort in knowing that by furthering the cause of authentic mourning now, we are not only living better lives ourselves, but we are also helping create a healthier world for the generations to come.

FINDING THE COURAGE TO BE VULNERABLE IN GRIEF

Given the lingering stigmas about authentic grief and mourning, it takes courage to be congruent and vulnerable in grief.

What is courage? When you think of courage, images of bravery might come to mind—knights on horseback charging their foe, firefighters risking their lives to rescue a family from a burning building, or hikers summiting Mount Everest. Yet this is bravery, not courage. Bravery is confident and outward.

Courage is quiet and inward. Without the steady, quiet resolve and unfailing commitment of courage, bravery would never happen. Courage is what fuels bravery. It is the bridge between fear and action. It is the still, quiet voice inside you encouraging you to go on.

As you work on adopting a vulnerable orientation in grief, you will need to find ways to befriend courage. Imagine what it would be like to have courage as a friend who walked beside you at all times—a friend who never nags, never pushes, but simply places a gentle hand on your back and whispers words of encouragement, helping you take the next step, and then the next.

I encourage you to cultivate a relationship with courage. Each morning, welcome courage. Before you rise, say your favorite quote on courage out loud. Maybe it is the Serenity Prayer, written by the theologian Reinhold Niebuhr: "God, grant me the serenity to accept the things I cannot change, the courage to change the things I can, and the wisdom to know the difference." Or maybe there's a different maxim that you especially like. If you want, write down your favorite quotes on courage and put them on your phone, fridge, dashboard, or mirror. They will help you keep courage close, all day long.

Next, consider what makes you feel fearful about the prospect of being open and honest in expressing your grief. Are you afraid of losing control, whether in public or in private? Do you have certain feelings that you are ashamed of or that are hard to talk about? Are you someone who has never learned to be outwardly emotional? Do you have friends and family members who don't know how to be present to emotionality and expressions of grief?

Whatever your apprehensions about authentic mourning may be, try mustering the courage to tackle them in tiny steps, one day at a time. Think of your grief as filling a secret room inside of you. Your task is to open the door to that room just a little bit at first, working your way up to, eventually, throwing the door wide open.

For example, if you are afraid of losing control in front of others, consider first thinking through on paper the thoughts and feelings you most need to express right now. In other words, start by writing them down. Writing is a form of mourning because it is expressing your thoughts outside of you. After you make notes, resolve to share some aspect of what you've written down with one other person. Be just a little vulnerable. You don't need to share everything all at once. (In fact, learning to disclose appropriately is an art we'll talk about on page 31.)

PRACTICING VULNERABILITY IN GRIEF AND MOURNING

So just how does one practice vulnerability in grief and mourning? What are the techniques and tactics? What do you need to "do"?

Other than being honest and transparent, there are no rules to practicing vulnerability in grief. There are no right or wrong ways to authentically mourn. What vulnerable mourning looks like for you in any given circumstance or on any given day will be a function of your unique life history, personality, cultural environment, and more.

Still, I thought it would be helpful to provide some vulnerable mourning ideas to help you get started.

• *Let your thoughts and feelings guide you.*
One of my main principles of healing in grief is that if something is

- bothering you

- weighing on you

- making you especially shocked/sad/anxious/angry/guilty (or any feeling)

- making you feel stuck

that means it's teaching you that it needs attention and expression.

Right now, when you allow yourself to think about and feel your grief, what bubbles to the surface most strongly? And what makes you feel most vulnerable when you imagine expressing it outside of yourself? Whatever that is, it's time to share it in some way.

Remember, your grief thoughts and feelings have a purpose. They exist to help you make the essential transition from life before the loss to life after the loss. Your most vulnerable, difficult thoughts and feelings are probably the most important ones to encounter and embrace. They are often the ones most meaningful to you. So, work on watching for them, welcoming them, and giving them voice as they naturally arise each day.

• *Put your feelings into words.*
If you are reticent to mourn openly and authentically, or unsure how to begin, consider starting by writing down your thoughts and feelings. You can use a journal, a loose piece of paper, a notes app on your phone, a computer file—it doesn't matter which writing tools you use.

Not only is writing a more private and thus safer-feeling method of mourning, but it also helps you clarify your own thoughts and feelings, and it helps you be vulnerable with yourself. It can be easy to avoid or deny the most tender aspects of your own grief. However, when you make the commitment to express them in writing, you are taking an important first step toward honesty and vulnerability.

• *Tell one thing to one other person.*
Try talking to your most empathetic, nonjudgmental friend about a specific grief thought or feeling that's been troubling you. Commit to yourself to tell them one thing you've thus far been afraid to express aloud, then see how they respond. Usually mourners find that any thoughts and feelings they've been holding back for fear of sounding abnormal or foolish are not only understood but in fact shared by others.

After you express this one thing and perhaps spend a few minutes discussing it with your friend, notice how you feel. Do you feel lighter? Easier in your body? A little more relaxed? In my work with grieving people, I typically find that one small, successful instance of sharing leads to more sharing. That's because vulnerability is, broadly speaking, its own reward.

• *Respond authentically to the question, "How are you doing?"*
In the weeks and months after someone has suffered a loss, when we run into them, we often ask them how they're doing. The standard answer is something blandly generic like, "Oh, I'm OK," or, "Hanging in there."

But now that you're working on mourning more authentically, I'd like you to consider giving a more honest, vulnerable response to this question. The next time someone asks you how you're doing, tell them the truth. You don't need to give a lengthy answer if you don't want to, and you don't have to get highly emotional (though it's absolutely OK if you do). Instead, I suggest that you try expressing one genuine challenge about your current grief experience.

For example, if you're struggling with low energy, say that. Or if the birthday of someone who died is coming up and you're apprehensive about it, mention that. Whatever is on your mind and heart, share at least a little of it. You'll find that most people are glad to have something specific to talk about. They may not know how to handle Grief with a capital G, but they can often navigate a discussion about a particular challenge or issue, and in that context offer a bit of empathy and support.

• *Every day, do one thing that scares you a little.*
I've talked about how vulnerability feels like fear. This is especially true when you're a vulnerability beginner. So if you're at least a little apprehensive about openly and fully expressing your grief outwardly, that's normal.

Each day, think about expressing your grief in some way. Of your choices, which make you feel that twinge of vulnerability? Pick one of those, and take at least a small step toward it.

Let's say you're grieving a death and have been meaning to talk to someone else affected by the loss…but the idea of that conversation, which will probably be painful, makes you feel vulnerable in anticipation. Take action by starting small. Today, just reach out to the person. Perhaps text or phone them and let them know you're thinking about them and would like to get together sometime. From there, the meeting can unfold naturally.

• *Wear your heart on your sleeve.*
Just as the Victorians wore black armbands when they were in mourning, I often advocate to mourners that wearing a button, piece of jewelry, or other symbol of their loss invites conversation and support from others.

Some time ago I created a lapel pin that reads, "Under Reconstruction." People who have suffered a shattering loss are working on putting the pieces back together. They are under reconstruction. Whenever they wear this pin, others often ask them what it means. This creates an opening for them to talk about their loss.

Consider wearing a symbol of your loss. It could be a pin or an awareness ribbon representing a certain illness or cause. It could be a photo button. It could be a necklace, an armband, an article of clothing, or a tattoo. This outward sign of your loss presents to the world that you are ready and willing to discuss something that is deeply important to you—and why.

• *Actively remember.*

In grief, contrary to popular belief, it's necessary to go backward before you can go forward. Spending quality time unearthing and reviewing memories is central to going backward.

Set aside a few minutes once or twice a week to go through photos, videos, and memorabilia associated with your loss. Sharing memories and anecdotes with a good listener—maybe someone who also has memories of this person or thing to share—is another way to actively remember.

As you remember and share your memories, you will naturally begin to piece together anecdotes of your love and loss. This process helps you build a narrative—an overarching story with a beginning, middle, and end. Stories carry meaning, so as you develop your story, you will naturally encounter realizations and opportunities for you to decide on what the events mean to you.

Don't forget to be vulnerable in your memory work. Allow yourself to explore memories and circumstances that might be painful or frightening (although traumatic memories are often best encountered with the help of a trained counselor). Be honest with yourself. Don't skip over the hard parts. Everything belongs, and all of it is part of your story of love and loss.

• *Partner up with a vulnerability buddy.*

Studies show that people are more likely to follow through with physical-activity commitments when they've promised to exercise with a friend. You can do the same with your mourning.

If you know someone else who is grieving and would also benefit from a vulnerability practice, invite them to get together. Just the two of you meeting regularly to talk honestly and openly about your losses will help a lot. But in addition, you can also discuss the concept of vulnerability and challenge one another to take more vulnerable mourning actions in between meetings.

• *Carry out grief rituals.*

Grief rituals are among the most powerful mourning actions you can take. They are "doing something" with your grief outside of yourself, so they count as mourning—even if you're doing them by yourself. Funerals are an example of a formal grief ritual, but you can come up with myriad informal ways to make grief rituals part of your regular routine.

For example, if someone you love has died, you might choose to talk out loud to a photo of that person each morning when you wake up. You could hold the photo as you tell them what your grief feels like at that moment as well as fill them in on your plans for the day. You could close with a statement of your intention for that day, such as "Today I'm going to work on reaching out to others, because I've been shutting them out too much and living with a protective orientation to my grief."

Other grief rituals might include combining elements such as playing a certain spiritual song or reciting a prayer, holding an object associated with your loss, and doing a physical action like walking a particular path or lighting a candle in remembrance. You can structure brief grief rituals that feel right to you.

Grief rituals invite vulnerability because their very purpose is to engage with and express your grief, bit by bit. During the ritual, you are dedicating your time and attention to the loss. You are acknowledging, thinking, feeling, and remembering. This creates a sweet spot of time-limited vulnerability held up by the structure of the ritual. You dose yourself with the work of authentic mourning, then you go about your day.

• *Join a support group.*
Grief support groups are vulnerability groups. That is, they're a designated place in which to take off any masks you may normally wear and allow yourself to experience and speak aloud your truest thoughts and feelings about the loss.

In the safety of a well-run group, you will find the freedom and support you need to be fully vulnerable. You won't need to pretend. You won't need to keep yourself "in control." You won't need to worry about looking foolish. After all, the whole point of the group is to bring together people who share the common bond of experience, to normalize and offer each other empathy.

Some introverted grieving people attend support groups but don't share a lot. If that's what happens for you, it can still be helpful. You will still learn about the healing benefits of open expression and mutual support. Whatever you do share will be valuable. And you may build connections with others that can last far beyond the time you're participating in the group.

• *Ask for and accept support from others.*
One of the most challenging things for many grievers to do is ask for help. After all, we've been conditioned by our cultural bias toward rugged individualism and the other grief-avoidant conventions on the left side of the chart. So we tend to see asking for or even accepting help as revealing weakness or burdening others.

Plus, it does take vulnerability to receive support. It means admitting we are not capable of coping and healing on our own. It means admitting we aren't fully self-sufficient.

But of course we're not fully self-sufficient. That's not how living as a human being works! We are built for social interaction and interdependence. Our greatest gift—love—

is the very essence of interdependence with others. Which is why I'm writing and you're reading this book! Because love has led to loss which has led to grief and the need to authentically mourn.

Just as vulnerability is a strength, so, too, are reaching out for help and accepting it when it's offered. The next time someone says to let them know if there's anything they can do for you, be ready to give them a suggestion. Maybe you'd like to get together for coffee to ease your loneliness. Maybe you need help with something practical, such as packing up belongings or figuring out paperwork. Or maybe you just need a hug at that very moment.

You are doing neither yourself nor others a favor when you avoid or reject their presence, words or gifts of sympathy, physical touch, and acts of service. Instead, choose to model vulnerability and mutual support by accepting such overtures. And when you're not getting the empathy and support you need, ask for it. It's OK if you are the one who initiates connection. Living on the right side of the chart requires proactive outreach. Give it a try and see what happens.

WHEN BEING VULNERABLE CAUSES MORE PAIN
Inherent to the practice of vulnerability is risk. That's what vulnerability is—presenting yourself honestly and openly to the outside world so that you are living your truth…and doing

so with the awareness that you can't control how the outside world will respond.

In general, the practice of vulnerability enhances connection and intimacy with others. It's how friendships are formed and bonds made stronger. But because not everyone is enlightened about the need for and benefits of vulnerability, you will still encounter many people living on the left side of the chart on page 10. You will still likely have friends and family members in the third of people who may be toxic to your mourning.

When your efforts to authentically mourn are met with anger, derision, judgment, scorn, mocking, avoidance, or misunderstanding, you may understandably be hurt. You may feel let down, foolish, or defeated. It's not a great feeling. If this happens to you, I'm sorry.

But the bigger promise of vulnerable grief and mourning is that overall, it's still the best path forward. Your intention is to be your authentic self and live your authentic truth. If others don't respond well to who you authentically are, that's on them. They clearly have their own self-exploration and growth to work on.

Still, I realize that such encounters can be painful, especially when the people responding poorly are colleagues, close friends, or family members. What should you do in these cases? You generally can't or shouldn't shut them out of your life. I encourage you to take the high road, if possible, and give them more time and space to learn and grow. In other words, have grace! In the meantime, try reserving your vulnerable expressions for those who can respond with empathy and hope. You deserve support and understanding. You deserve unconditional love.

MONITOR YOUR SHARING

I have found that some grieving people are reticent to share their grief because they don't want to burden or bother other people. These grievers are typically introverts who need help understanding that other people want to be bothered! Virtually everyone desires connection and intimacy in their lives. If you're an introvert or someone who's emotionally guarded, taking baby steps toward vulnerable sharing will help you discover the power of vulnerability.

Conversely, some grieving people tend to overshare their grief. People who overshare their emotions and internal monologue often make their friends and family uncomfortable or wear out their welcome—leading to less connection and intimacy, not more.

Keep in mind that vulnerability is only vulnerability when it feels tender and special. What's more, good relationships require balance and mutual support. If you're not sure if you're practicing healthy self-disclosure or if you're oversharing, ask someone you know who has healthy emotionality and communication to help you determine if you're routinely talking too much, repeating yourself, giving too many details, or otherwise dominating interactions. If you are, part of your vulnerability practice will be working on placing healthy boundaries on your own self-disclosure.

BALANCING VULNERABILITY AND RESILIENCE

Thanks to resilience, you're still here. You've suffered a terrible loss, and you're surviving.

Like positivity, resilience can also be toxic, especially in our grief-avoidant culture. Beware of resilience that lives on the left side of the chart. It may tell you to "suck it up," "let go," and put your loss behind you. It may suggest that you need to be strong and in control.

Yet the practice of vulnerability is teaching you to embrace all your thoughts and feelings, and give them the time and attention they deserve. It's teaching you to relinquish the illusion of control over your grief. In a sense, this means surrendering to something that is greater than you. Instead of thinking you always have to understand your grief, allow yourself to stand under your grief.

As time passes, I encourage you to both practice vulnerability and cultivate healthy resilience. Think of them as the two sides of a seesaw. You want the seesaw to balance sometimes, yes, but you also want it to go up and down. On some days you will need to open yourself to your naturally painful grief. The vulnerable side of the seesaw will tilt down. On other days you will allow your resilience to help you navigate new challenges and approach life openly as it moves toward you. The resilient side of the seesaw will tilt down.

Mourning requires you to be vulnerable to your deepest pain and your most challenging thoughts and feelings. It asks you to encounter them fully and express whatever they bring up for you. It asks you not to suppress or deny or distract but instead to immerse. This immersion is necessary because it is the truth.

But here comes resilience! And resilience asks you to dose yourself with your grief and mourning. It says, "Yes, encounter your necessary grief for a while, then let's go engage in life for a while. We'll keep going like that, back and forth, back and forth." This is healthy resilience.

It's this back-and-forth of grief, in fact, that provides momentum for the journey. I also call it evade-encounter. It's healthy to take part in non-grief-focused activities part of the time (though your loss always lives inside you). It's healthy to evade your grief sometimes. Then it's also healthy, and necessary, to return to regularly encounter your grief.

Imagine one of those old-fashioned handcars that railroad workers used in the 1800s and 1900s to traverse train tracks. Two people would stand on either side of the handcar's small platform, and by taking turns pumping the seesaw-like lever back and forth, back and forth, they could quickly convey themselves down the track with their own muscle power.

The handcar metaphor captures the reciprocating power of evade-encounter in grief as well as vulnerability and resilience. When you consciously activate and rely on both as you journey through grief, and you work to keep them in healthy balance, you create divine momentum toward healing. However, if you neglect one side or the other, you get stuck, and you go nowhere.

The Wikipedia entry on handcars says, "While depictions on TV and in movies might suggest that being a member of a handcar crew was a joyride, in fact pumping a traditional handcar…could be very hard work." Likewise, the back-and-forth of resilience and vulnerability in grief are very hard work. Remind yourself that there are no rewards for speed. If your handcar moves very slowly, so be it. If it goes backward sometimes, so be it. As long as it's moving, you're on the right track.

WORKING TOWARD RECONCILIATION

As you work on your vulnerability practice—authentically

mourning in doses each day, one day at a time—you are working toward reconciliation of your grief. Grief never truly ends, but through authentic mourning it softens over time, and eventually your loss becomes an integrated part of your life story.

You began this journey from a place of brokenheartedness. Of course your heart was broken. You lost someone or some thing precious to you. That is a life-shattering experience. But then the question became, "What do I do with this broken heart?" And you are finding the courage to answer by picking up the pieces in vulnerable ways— ways that bring connection, hope, and meaning to your life—and slowly stitch them back together again.

Your ultimate goal is wholeheartedness. Your reconciled heart will be a patchwork heart, to be sure. But the more open, honest, expressive, congruent, and present you are each day, the more wholehearted you will become.

According to Brené Brown, an American research professor and popular speaker and author, wholehearted people believe in living with courage, compassion, and connection. They make themselves vulnerable and open because they value authenticity. Instead of resisting change and the sometimes chaotic nature of life, they learn to surrender to whatever is happening that may be outside their control. They develop the skills of living in the moment and healthy positivity. They find beauty and meaning in imperfection, doing and being and loving the best they can.

Some of you may be doubting your ability to become wholehearted again. To have doubts is not unusual when you are brokenhearted. At various points on the path to reconciliation, you may find yourself exhausted and in despair. Your quest for healing is so hard—maybe the hardest thing you've ever done. It's normal to want to give up now and then.

Others of you may be having a hard time mustering the desire to work toward wholeheartedness. You may be so deep in the wound of your grief that you don't have the energy to climb out. Besides, you may ask, isn't the idea of wholeheartedness wishful thinking?

I assure you that reconciliation and wholeheartedness are within your reach. I have borne witness to grieving people as they worked through their mourning countless times. I have absolutely no doubt that you, too, have the capacity to become wholehearted again.

FOSTERING HOPE

Hope is also essential to the honest, vulnerable orientation to life and grief. Hope is an expectation of a good that is yet to be. Unlike toxic positivity, it doesn't deny painful truths. Hope is what rallies energies and activates the courage to allow you to commit to authentic mourning. Hope lives alongside grief, bearing witness to the loss and the hurt while at the same time knowing that there are also good things to come. Yes, out of the dark comes light.

Vulnerability is not all doom and gloom. Neither is it solely about touchy-feely conversation and self-disclosure. It can also be buoyant and bubbly. It can include forays into passions and new adventures. Vulnerability can be exciting, even thrilling.

In grief, hope imbues vulnerability with a sense of promise. As you work on your vulnerability practice, you can simultaneously work to foster hope. Whenever you can, consider all the possible goods that may yet be in your life. Perhaps touch on them in your conversations with others. Look into the things that excite you, and begin to add them to your life. When you find you are ready, commit yourself to authentically mourn in ways that eventually lead to your hope for healing.

PART THREE:

LIVING INSIDE OUT

"Vulnerability is the only authentic state. Being vulnerable means being open, for wounding, but also for pleasure. Being open to the wounds of life means also being open to the bounty and beauty."

— Stephen Russell

Over the long run, practicing vulnerability can become a way of life. And what a freeing, enriching way to live.

As someone whose calling and long career have been centered on the practice of open emotionality, I can assure you that the rewards of vulnerability are far, far greater than any risks. I know my own life would be a mere shadow of what it is had I not realized at a young age that denying and suppressing difficult feelings only thwarts true living. And I have been privileged to witness the lives of countless people be transformed for the better by the hard work of authentic mourning.

You, too, can make the courageous but worthwhile choice to live inside out from here forward.

VULNERABILITY IS OUR TRUE NATURE

We are all born vulnerable. It is our nature to be open and to freely allow experiences to flow in and thoughts and feelings to flow out.

If you've ever watched a young child navigate the world, you've seen how genuine and loving they are. We say they are "innocent." By this we mean that they have not yet been contaminated by cultural conventions. It's a beautiful thing.

It is only as children grow and learn society's harmful rules—the ones on the left side of the chart on page 10—that they begin to don the armor of denial, stoicism, and separation.

But what is learned can be unlearned. Even for the most well-seasoned among us, it's not too late to take steps to reclaim our true selves. Let's all work on peeling off any façades so we can once again experience the full breadth of unreserved living and loving.

VULNERABILITY IS POWER

The more you practice vulnerability, the more you will realize that vulnerability isn't weakness—it's power.

Vulnerability is unguarded and unaffected. That is, it doesn't try to posture or pretend. When you are practicing vulnerability, you are simply being you—without pretense, affectation, or defensiveness.

The Vulnerability of Grief

In the beginning of this book, I said that vulnerability typically feels like fear. But here's a secret: as you get better at living vulnerably, it will begin to feel like the strength that it is. As you begin to experience the many advantages of allowing yourself to be vulnerable, you will likely never turn back. That is how positively transformative the practice of vulnerability can be.

You will probably find that those among your friends and family who are unaccustomed to such authenticity won't know what to make of it (especially if you're someone who's thus far been more guarded with your emotionality). They may be surprised, even shocked. They might be put off or get upset. They may actually think you're losing your mind.

But one of the powers of vulnerability is that it tends to wear down the defenses of others. Whether they're consciously aware of it or not, human beings actually crave authenticity. People will notice that you're opening up. They will see that you're exposing your most tender self. And in return, many of them will venture to do the same in your presence. That is why vulnerability has such amazing powers of connection. It often deepens relationships, strengthens loyalties, and reinforces bonds.

Vulnerability also has the power to help you recognize and reach toward your hopes and dreams. When you're living on the left side of the chart, you're often suppressing your true desires because they may seem foolish to you or unacceptable to others. You're wearing the armor of social custom. You're practicing perfectionism, which doesn't allow you to get out there, get messy, and make mistakes.

But the practice of vulnerability helps reacquaint you with your true self. If you have any long-dormant passions or yearnings, they may well reemerge. With your newfound understanding of the benefits of taking risks and making mistakes, you may find it easier to begin to explore those passions and yearnings. After all, why not? Life is short. You realize that the only real risk is dying with unexplored passions and yearnings still inside you.

In these ways, vulnerability also builds self-worth. It's not a boastful, ego-driven type of self-worth, either. Instead, it's genuine and life-affirming. It says, "I'm privileged to be here, and while I am, I'm going to be me. I'm going to experience everything I'm pulled to experience, and build meaning and connection every precious day that's given to me." What is more powerful than that?

VULNERABLE LIVING

What does it mean to live "inside out"? To me it means engaging in each moment with authenticity, kindness, and hope. Here are some ways to integrate vulnerability into your living and loving.

• *Vulnerability in your attention to self*
As you go through your day, pay attention to what your body, mind, and soul are telling you. For example, are you getting hungry? Is your energy low? Are you feeling happy and joyful? Are you distracted?

On a day-to-day basis, practicing vulnerability with yourself simply means maintaining an honest awareness of how you're doing, then responding with loving, appropriate self-care. It can also mean advocating for yourself when needed. If you're tired, you rest. If you're feeling happy, you celebrate and express your happiness.

On a longer timeline, practicing vulnerability with yourself means attending to your long-term needs and goals. You regularly make time to consider what you really want in order to give your life joy and meaning. And then you take steps to explore those directions and achieve your goals. This includes career, hobbies, family planning, recreation, and more. Along the way, you are always rechecking in with yourself and noticing if your goals are evolving. Just because you wanted something five years ago doesn't have to mean you want it now.

Not only is a vulnerable orientation to self fluid, it also

encourages experimentation and growth. You realize it's good to try new things, put yourself out there, and make mistakes. In fact, playing it overly safe in order to avoid embarrassment or failure often results in missing out on the countless wonders of life. This doesn't mean you need to be reckless or irresponsible. It just means that when you're curious about something, you allow yourself to be vulnerable and explore it.

• *Vulnerability in your relationships*
We've already discussed how vulnerability in relationships requires being open and honest about your grief, which in turn builds connection and intimacy. It really is the key that strengthens bonds and loyalties.

More broadly, practicing vulnerability in relationships requires openness and honesty about everything. You monitor your sharing to ensure that the relationship remains balanced, and you don't expect any one person to meet all your needs. Beyond that, you are simply yourself around others. You practice congruency. You express how you feel. You let your instincts guide you.

You also remember that all relationships are reciprocal. True vulnerability is not anchored in aggressiveness. The ego is set aside. You are always mindful of communicating and relating in a manner that treats the vulnerabilities of others with gentle respect. Just as you are kind to yourself, you are kind to others.

- *Vulnerability in your communities*

To be vulnerable in your communities is to serve them with your natural strengths and gifts. If you care about something, you help nurture it. If you're concerned about something, you help fix it. That's one important way in which you live your truth.

What gives your life meaning? What brings you a sense of purpose? Whatever your answers to these questions are, you look to your communities to help support these activities or causes. If your career is a calling, you engage fully because it's something important to you. Outside of your job, you might volunteer your time and talents as a way of furthering your passions in the world. Conversely, you also practice vulnerability in your communities by disengaging with any activities or groups that no longer feel congruent to you. You remember that vulnerability is always honest, and so you rely on authenticity to guide you.

THE VULNERABLE ORIENTATION TO LIFE

PROTECTIVE, DISHONEST ORIENTATION	HONEST, VULNERABLE ORIENTATION
We put on a false front.	We present ourselves to the world as we really are, warts and all.
We don't divulge our truest feelings.	We share our truest feelings openly and proactively.
We keep a stiff upper lip.	We allow ourselves to be sad and emotional when feelings arise.
We don't share our more tender emotions.	We share all our emotions, including the tender ones.
We don't ask for everything we truly want and need.	We feel comfortable and empowered to ask for everything we truly want and need.
We avoid candor and closeness.	We are always genuine, which brings us closer to others.
We run away from intimacy.	We move toward intimacy.
We retreat to numbness, stoicism, and denial.	We choose tenderness, expression, and truth-seeking.
We practice perfectionism.	We are human, and we make mistakes. We live with a growth mindset and generously forgive mistakes in ourselves and others.
We champion resilience over vulnerability.	We know that vulnerability is essential to true resilience.
We adopt toxic positivity, paste on a smile, and "carry on."	We cultivate hope while still giving our full attention to difficult experiences and feelings as they arise.

MY IDEAS FOR LIVING HONESTLY AND VULNERABLY

A FINAL WORD

"Let your heart crumble into an infinite amount of tiny, precious seeds. Then plant love everywhere you go."
— Anita Krizzan

Your brokenheartedness is a testament to your love. As you discover ways to authentically mourn, day by day, you are stitching your broken heart back together so you can once again live wholeheartedly.

But I also like this metaphor of a grieving heart crumbling into seeds that can be sown as love wherever you go.

Practicing vulnerability in grief and in life is, in essence, the practice of sowing love:

- love for the people and things you've lost
- love for yourself
- love for your friends and family
- love for your communities
- love for the world
- love for your deepest beliefs and passions

Thank you for joining me in this exploration about the vulnerability of grief. Today I challenge you to muster the courage to authentically mourn in some small way. Tomorrow I challenge you to do the same.

I hope we meet one day, and if we do, I hope you will tell me about your journey into vulnerability and authentic mourning. By living inside out, you are revealing yourself to be the beautiful miracle you always were inside.

ABOUT THE AUTHOR

Alan D. Wolfelt, Ph.D., is a respected author and educator on the topics of companioning others and healing in grief. He serves as Director of the Center for Loss and Life Transition and is on the faculty at the University of Colorado Medical

School's Department of Family Medicine. Dr. Wolfelt has written many bestselling books on healing in grief, including *Understanding Your Grief, Healing Your Grieving Heart*, and *Grief One Day at a Time*. Visit www.centerforloss.com to learn more about grief and loss and to order Dr. Wolfelt's books.

The Hope and Healing Series
Concise books of wisdom and comfort

Readers and counselors often ask Dr. Wolfelt to write books on specialized topics not well-covered elsewhere in the grief literature. He created the Hope and Healing Series to fulfill their requests. These short books focus in on particular types of loss and aspects of grief that while distinct, are not uncommon. They affect many millions of people worldwide, each of whom deserves affirmation, support, and guidance for their unique circumstances.

All Dr. Wolfelt's publications can be ordered by mail from:
Companion Press, 3735 Broken Bow Road, Fort Collins, CO 80526
(970) 226-6050 • www.centerforloss.com

First Aid for Broken Hearts

Life is both wonderful and devastating. It graces us with joy, and

it breaks our hearts. If your heart is broken, this book is for you.

Loss may be an unavoidable part of human life, but it doesn't have to prevent you from living well. You can and will survive this. Actually, if you adopt this guide's basic principles, revealed and tested by Dr. Wolfelt, you will even go on to thrive.

ISBN 978-1-61722-281-8
118 pages • softcover • $9.95

All Dr. Wolfelt's publications can be ordered by mail from:
Companion Press, 3735 Broken Bow Road, Fort Collins, CO 80526
(970) 226-6050 • www.centerforloss.com

Understanding Your Grief [SECOND EDITION]

This book is Dr. Wolfelt's most comprehensive, covering the essential lessons that mourners have taught him in his four decades of

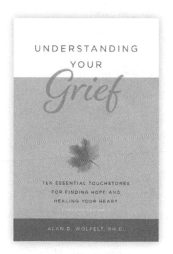

working with the bereaved. In compassionate, down-to-earth language, *Understanding Your Grief* describes ten touchstones—or trail markers—that are essential physical, emotional, cognitive, social, and spiritual signs for mourners to look for on their journey through grief.

Think of your grief as a wilderness— a vast, inhospitable forest. You must journey through this wilderness. In the wilderness of your grief, the touchstones are your trail markers.

They are the signs that let you know you are on the right path. When you learn to identify and rely on the touchstones, you will find your way to hope and healing.

ISBN 978-1-617223-07-5 • 240 pages • softcover • $14.95

All Dr. Wolfelt's publications can be ordered by mail from:
Companion Press, 3735 Broken Bow Road, Fort Collins, CO 80526
(970) 226-6050 • www.centerforloss.com

Loving from the Outside In, Mourning from the Inside Out

"The capacity to love requires the necessity to mourn," writes Dr. Wolfelt in this lovely gift book. "In other words, love and grief are

two sides of the same precious coin. One does not—and cannot—exist without the other. They are the yin and yang of our lives. What higher purpose is there in life but to give and receive love? Love is the essence of a life of abundance and joy. No matter what life brings our way, love is our highest goal, our most passionate quest. People sometimes say that grief is the price we pay for the joy of having loved. If we allow ourselves the grace that comes with love, we must allow ourselves the grace that is required to mourn."

In this compassionate guide, Dr. Wolfelt explores what love and grief have in common and invites the reader to mourn well in order to go on to live and love well again.

ISBN: 978-1-61722-147-7 • Price: $15.95 • 96 pages

All Dr. Wolfelt's publications can be ordered by mail from:
Companion Press, 3735 Broken Bow Road, Fort Collins, CO 80526
(970) 226-6050 • www.centerforloss.com

YOUR NOTES ON THE VULNERABILITY OF GRIEF

_____

_____

_____

_____

_____

_____

_____

_____

_____

_____

_____

_____

_____

_____

_____

_____

_____

_____

_____

_____

_____

YOUR NOTES ON THE VULNERABILITY OF GRIEF

YOUR NOTES ON THE VULNERABILITY OF GRIEF